Conflict at Work

By Daniel Barnett

The Employment Law Library

All books in the Employment Law Library are sent for free to members of the HR Inner Circle.

1. Employee Investigations
2. GDPR for HR Professionals
3. Preventing and Defending Employee Stress Claims
4. Employment Tribunal Time Limits
5. Deconstructing TUPE
6. Changing Terms & Conditions
7. Constructive Dismissal
8. Resolving Grievances
9. HR Hazards
10. Employment Status
11. Spotting Malingering
12. Employment Tribunal Compensation
13. Hiring Staff
14. Computer and Social Media Misuse
15. Managing Sickness Absence
16. The Three Ps
17. Conflict at Work
18. SOSR Dismissals

Published by Employment Law Services Limited, Unit 3, Chequers Farm, Chequers Lane, Watford, Hertfordshire WD25 0LG

Acknowledgments

This is book 17 in the series of mini-guides on employment law for HR professionals.

As always, there are people to thank. First and foremost, thanks to Becky Ranauta for her help with the content. Thanks also to Tincuta Collett for the layout and design, Aaron Gaff for proofreading and Maria Rodriguez for converting the book into the formats needed for Amazon.

None of these books are possible without the input and experience of all the members of the HR Inner Circle. I write these small books for you, and you get them for free as part of your membership (along with more help and support in your HR role than you can shake a stick at). I particularly want to thank Patrick McNamee, Michelle Dalby, Penelope Douglass, Claire Loftus, Tamasin Sutton and Natasha Kearslake, each of whom reviewed an early draft of this book and added valuable suggestions and insight.

If you're not a member and you're interested in learning more about HR Inner Circle membership (www.hrinnercircle.co.uk), there is some information at the back of this book.

Daniel Barnett
September 2023

ABOUT THE AUTHOR

 Daniel Barnett is a leading employment law barrister practising from Outer Temple Chambers. With 25 years' experience defending public and private sector employers against employment claims, he has represented a Royal Family, several international airlines, FTSE-100 companies and various NHS Trusts and local authorities. Employee clients include David & Victoria Beckham's nanny and Paul Mason (subject of the ITV documentary 'Britain's Fattest Man').

Daniel is a past chair of the Employment Lawyers' Association's publishing committee and electronic services working party. He is the author or co-author of eight books, including the Law Society Handbook on Employment Law (currently in its 8th edition). He is the creator of the Employment Law (UK) mailing list, an email alerter bulletin service sending details of breaking news in employment law three times a week to 30,000 recipients.

Legal directories describe him as 'extremely knowledgeable and [he] can absorb pages of instructions at lightning speed', 'involved in a number of highly contentious matters', 'singled out for his work for large blue-chip companies', 'combination of in-depth legal knowledge, pragmatism, quick response times and approachability', 'inexhaustible', 'tenacious', 'knowledgeable', and 'an excellent advocate'.

He is one of the leading speakers and trainers on the employment law and HR circuit. He has presented seminars for the House of Commons, the BBC, Oxford University, HSBC, Barclays Bank, Ocado, and dozens of other organisations in-house. In 2013, 2014, 2016, and 2019 he designed — and was the sole speaker at — the Employment Law MasterClass national tour.

As well as full-time practice as a barrister and speaker, Daniel is the founder of the HR Inner Circle – a membership club for smart, ambitious HR Professionals. In 2007, he co-founded CPD Webinars Ltd, then the UK's leading webinar training company for lawyers, and sold it to Thomson Reuters in 2011.

Daniel is widely sought after as a commentator in both broadcast and print media on all legal issues. Since 2010 he has presented the Legal Hour on LBC Radio. In 2019, he launched Employment Law Matters, a weekly podcast with short explanations of employment law topics. Subscribe at www.danielbarnett.co.uk/podcast

www.danielbarnett.co.uk
Outer Temple Chambers
Strand, London

Contents

Chapter 1:   Causes and types of conflict   13

Chapter 2:   The impact of
              conflict on staff   31

Chapter 3:   Resolving conflict   37

Chapter 4:   Preventing future conflict   71

Introduction

We would all like to work in an environment where everyone gets on famously with their colleagues and teams work together like a well-oiled machine.

Unfortunately, human nature does not generally allow for this, and at times, a working environment is more of a battleground than a professional, calm and supportive workplace.

On the upside, it means that HR or employee relations teams at least, will always be needed.

On the downside, negative conflict is disruptive and expensive. The full scale of the financial impact of workplace conflict was calculated by Acas in its May 2021 'Estimating the costs of workplace conflict' report. The report found that conflict costs UK organisations £28.5 billion a year, which is the equivalent of more than £1,000 per employee and more than the GDP of Malta.

Unsurprisingly, the conclusion of Acas's report was that prevention is better than cure. The earlier intervention takes place and conflicts are addressed, the less likely an employer is to find itself dealing with (and paying for) the fall-out.

This book explores the causes and impact of conflict, including the potential legal claims that can arise, before looking at ways to resolve it. The book also addresses ways in which you can seek to eradicate and prevent negative conflict.

CHAPTER 1
Causes and types of conflict

Workplace conflict can occur in different ways. It can be obvious, like a heated argument, or less visible, like excluding someone from a work social event. It is, rightly, the most serious incidents, such as bullying and harassment, that are often given the most attention. However, it is important to keep in mind that even a seemingly minor disagreement can fester and spiral upwards into serious conflict if left unchecked. The Chartered Institute of Personnel and Development (CIPD) in its 2020 report, 'Managing conflict in the modern workplace', found that 26% of employees considered that conflict was a 'common occurrence' at work, and 35% said they had experienced some form of interpersonal conflict – either an isolated dispute or ongoing difficult relationship – over the previous year. The single most common cause of conflict in the report was 'differences in personality styles or working', closely followed by 'individual competence and performance'. Most often, such incidences of conflict take place between colleagues in a team or with their manager.

The real problems come when the innocent-sounding 'difference in personality styles' or 'performance issues' tip over into more serious types of conflict.

Bullying and harassment

One of the best-known sources of workplace conflict is bullying and harassment. The terms 'bullying' and 'harassment' are often bundled together to describe certain patterns of behaviour. However, legally, they are distinct, which impacts how any incidents should be unpicked and dealt with.

Harassment – Equality Act

The profile of sexual harassment has been particularly raised in recent years due to movements such as #MeToo, but this is by no means the only form of harassment in the workplace. It extends to the majority of 'protected characteristics' defined under the *Equality Act 2010*, including a person's age, disability, gender reassignment, race, religion or belief, sexual orientation and sex (which also covers pregnancy). Also, similar to other forms of discrimination, all staff and job applicants are protected. It is only the genuinely self-employed who are not.

The definition of harassment is set out at section 26 of the *Equality Act 2010*:

"A person (A) harasses another (B) if A engages in unwanted conduct related to a relevant protected

characteristic, which has the purpose or effect of either
violating B's dignity or creating an intimidating, hostile,
degrading, humiliating or offensive environment for B."

Further, the *Equality Act 2010* sets out a definition of
sexual harassment:

"A engages in unwanted conduct of a sexual nature
which has the purpose or effect of violating B's dignity or
creating an intimidating, hostile, degrading, humiliating or
offensive environment for B."

This means there must be actual sexual content or
connotation, for example, making sexual remarks or
jokes, or making promotion decisions on the basis of
sexual advances being accepted or rejected.

Finally, the *Equality Act 2010* defines sex (or gender
reassignment)-related harassment:

"A engages in unwanted conduct that is related to sex or
gender reassignment, which has the purpose or effect of
violating B's dignity or creating an intimidating, hostile,
degrading, humiliating or offensive environment for B
and/or because of B's rejection of or submission to the
conduct, A treats B less favourably than A would treat B if
B had not rejected or submitted to the conduct."

This form of harassment is not sexual in nature but is
behaviour that is linked in some way to gender and
causes offence to an individual.

For example, where an employee is constantly telling derogatory or demeaning jokes about either women or men and an individual (male or female) finds this unwelcome and offensive, or where a manager gives a junior female employee a poor performance review because she has consistently knocked back his repeated advances.

An important point to remember when dealing with harassment (or any other form of discrimination) is that under section 109 of the *Equality Act 2010*, the employer is likely to be held liable for the actions of its staff. This is the case even when an employer has no knowledge or approval of the discriminatory conduct. This means the junior female colleague who was given a poor performance review because she had rejected a male manager's sexual advances could bring an employment tribunal claim for sex discrimination against her employer. The only way in which the employer will be able to defend itself and escape liability is if it can show that it took all 'reasonable steps' to prevent the manager from acting in a discriminatory manner. Such reasonable steps will normally include:

- Having an equal opportunities policy, perhaps alongside a more detailed anti-harassment and bullying policy, which is reviewed regularly and communicated to all staff

- Training managers on equal opportunities and harassment

- Dealing properly with complaints and disciplining anyone who is found to have engaged in such conduct

Another legal claim to be aware of is that of 'victimisation'. An employer can be liable for this under the *Equality Act 2010* if it mistreats an employee who has raised or been involved in allegations of discrimination or harassment. The protection is pretty wide. One of the examples given in the Equality and Human Rights Commission's (EHRC's) Employment Statutory Code of Practice involves a senior manager who hears a worker's grievance about harassment. The manager finds that the worker has been harassed. The manager does the right thing and offers a formal apology, disciplines the employee responsible and signs them up for diversity training. However, the manager's reward for this best practice behaviour is to be reprimanded by his director who refuses to put him forward to attend an important conference on behalf of the company. This mistreatment of the manager by the director is likely to amount to victimisation of the manager.

However, the good news is that in one area, employers' liability for harassment has been reduced. There is nothing that imposes direct liability on an employer for third-party harassment, other than where the employer has failed to act on third-party harassment because of their own discriminatory motivation. The government proposed, in 2021, to legislate to re-introduce protection against third-party harassment, with an 'all reasonable steps' defence for employers. But due to opposition from employer's groups and the House of Lords, this proposal was dropped in summer 2023.

Harassment – the Protection from Harassment Act

In addition to claims under the *Equality Act 2010*, employees also have a potential claim against their employer under the *Protection from Harassment Act 1997*. However, this Act only applies to situations where there is a course of conduct rather than a one-off incident. There needs to be two or more linked incidents and these need to be unacceptable, oppressive and calculated to cause 'alarm, fear or distress'. The conduct also needs to be sufficiently serious to 'justify the sanctions of the criminal law'.

Given the hurdles to overcome in bringing a claim under the *Protection from Harassment Act 1997*, it is not greatly used by those employees who are already protected by discrimination laws. It is more widely used by those who have been harassed or bullied at work but cannot point to a protected characteristic to explain their treatment.

Bullying

According to the CIPD in its 2020 report, 'Managing conflict in the modern workplace', employees are almost twice as likely to say they have experienced bullying at work rather than harassment.

There is no legal definition of bullying, but Acas says it can include 'offensive, intimidating, malicious or insulting behaviour, an abuse or misuse of power through means that undermine, humiliate, denigrate or injure the recipient'.

The legal position regarding workplace bullying is more complex than it is regarding harassment because there's no single law that covers it. An employee who considers that they have been bullied will need to piece together their protection under a variety of different laws. This could include a claim for breach of an express or implied term of the employment contract, for example, breach of the implied term of trust and confidence.

If sufficiently serious, and if the employee has the required two years' continuous service, this could lead to a constructive unfair dismissal claim, for example, an employee who feels forced to leave their job because of an employer's failure to deal with their complaint about bullying.

An employee may also claim that by raising their complaint of bullying, they have made a protected disclosure or 'blown the whistle'. If they are mistreated as a result of such a complaint, it can lead to a successful claim against the employer under the *Public Interest Disclosure Act 1998*. However, to do so, the employee will need to show that their disclosure was made in the public interest. This means the incident of bullying would likely need to affect a group of people rather than just an individual. For example, the former Home Office Permanent Secretary Sir Philip Rutnam brought a tribunal claim for whistleblowing on the basis that he had been mistreated following his allegations about Home Secretary Priti Patel's alleged bullying. He argued that his disclosure was in the public interest because Priti Patel's alleged bullying was towards a number of members of staff, not just him.

Other claims that employees could bring include breach of an employer's duty to provide a safe workplace under the *Health and Safety at Work Act 1974* or common law. Also, if the bullying is sufficiently serious and more than a one-off incident, the employee could bring a claim under the *Protection from Harassment Act 1997*, referred to earlier.

Don't forget, also, that an employer may be liable for another employee's actions under the rules of 'vicarious liability'. This means that if an employee carries out a wrongful act that causes harm to another employee, the employer will be liable if that act is closely connected to the employment. For example, in *Green v DB Group Services Limited [2006] IRLR 764*, the High Court awarded £852,000 in damages to an employee who suffered bullying and harassment from fellow employees once she began a relationship with her head of department. The Court found that the employee had been subjected to a relentless campaign of 'mean and spiteful behaviour' by four female employees and to 'domineering, disrespectful, dismissive and confrontational' behaviour from a male co-worker. Despite the fact the four women did not work directly with Ms Green, the Court held there was a close connection between the women's employment and their behaviour towards her. Further, the employer knew, or ought to have known, about the bullying as it was a long-standing problem in the department. Instead, the employer's senior management had 'collectively closed their eyes' to it.

One highly relevant form of bullying in the modern age of hybrid working is 'cyberbullying'. This is where the bullying takes place online or using electronic devices, for example, through social media platforms, texts, apps and emails. It can include behaviour such as posting inappropriate pictures, sending offensive messages or threatening to reveal personal information online. When faced with cyberbullying, employees have open to them all the legal protections we have just discussed. Also, depending on the nature and severity of the conduct, it may be possible to involve the police – if only to manage reputations and ensure that everything is done to prevent further attacks. For example, action for a criminal offence can be taken under the *Malicious Communications Act 1988*. The Act states that it is an offence for any person to send a communication that is 'indecent or grossly offensive' with the intent of 'causing distress or anxiety to the recipient', and this includes threats and information that is false or known or believed to be false by the sender of the communication. Also, the

Communications Act 2003 states that it is a criminal offence to send comments electronically that are deemed 'grossly offensive or of an indecent, obscene or menacing character'. If found guilty under either of these Acts, a person can receive up to six months imprisonment, a fine or both.

Performance management

Although cyber-bullying is on the rise, it is still not as common as the staple source of conflict – that between a manager and members of their team. In fact, 40% of those surveyed for the CIPD's 2020 report, 'Managing conflict in the modern workplace', reported that their most recent experience of bullying was carried out by their manager. The roots are often based on performance issues and blamed on heavy-handed and overbearing managers. However, of course, there are two sides to every workplace story. One person's 'bullying, overbearing manager' could well be another's 'hard-working and diligent manager' trying their best to deal with an underperforming and work-shy employee.

Nevertheless, the unavoidable truth is that picking an employee up on their deficiencies can lead to conflict, which can get tricky to unravel. The most important thing for a manager to do here is to act reasonably. All the claims mentioned so far are at stake here. An unreasonable approach by a manager can quickly snowball into claims alleging abuse of power. One of the examples given in the EHRC's Employment Statutory Code of Practice is that of an employee of Somali origin who, after a dispute over an unreasonably harsh performance review, is subjected to disciplinary proceedings. The employee believes this step was inappropriate and unfair and brings a claim for direct race discrimination. If the behaviour of the manager is found to be atypical and different to how they would treat another team member, the employer is likely to be found liable for the manager's discriminatory behaviour.

Of course, it remains important that managers be allowed to do their job and achieve the goals their team has been set. Many employees no doubt confuse 'bullying' with firm management. It is not bullying for a manager to set performance goals, standards and deadlines, to allocate (or re-allocate) work between the team, to discuss unsatisfactory performance or inappropriate behaviour or to implement organisational change.

However, to avoid firm management tipping over into bullying, it is recommended that managers ask themselves the following questions:

- Are all comments, requests and criticisms constructive and fair?

- Is all criticism aimed at the mistake rather than the individual?

- Are there positive developmental intentions behind all criticism?

- Are the feelings of the individual taken into consideration?

The key principle for managers to consider when having difficult conversations with their staff is to stay objective and professional at all times. They should avoid it becoming personal and stay focused on developmental and positive work aims rather than individual character traits and perceived personality weaknesses.

It often comes down to treating people with dignity and respect. This is covered further in Chapter 4, which explores ways to prevent workplace conflict.

Personality clash

Sometimes, it is the employees within a team or company who just do not get on. Quite often, there isn't a specific issue or problem that causes the conflict; the employees just have incompatible personalities. This intangible quality makes personality clashes notoriously difficult issues to deal with.

The most challenging and high-stakes personality clashes can involve members of senior management. For example, in *Gallacher v Abellio Scotrail Limited UKEATS/0027/19*, the employee, Mrs Gallacher, was a senior manager. Over the course of her employment, her relationship with her line manager became strained as a result of various disputes relating predominantly to salary and recruitment issues. Mrs Gallacher started to openly make negative comments about her manager and was aggressive towards her. These long-standing issues came to a head when the employer began trading at a loss. This meant changes needed to be made quickly. As there were no signs that the relationship could be repaired and no alternative roles for the employee, the employer dismissed Mrs Gallacher without any disciplinary procedure. It did so in light of HR advice that the matter was not one of conduct or capability and that there was no process that could help manage the situation. Mrs Gallacher was not offered the right of appeal and was paid in lieu of her notice entitlement.

This case illustrates the difficulties in knowing what to do in situations where there is an irretrievable breakdown in relationships. Although it is generally advisable to avoid dismissing without following a process, it is not always obvious what the correct procedure is. In this case, the employer successfully persuaded the tribunal and the EAT that the dismissal was fair on the basis that following a formal procedure would have made the situation worse. In other words, any further attempts to repair the relationship would be futile and the consequences of the breakdown in the relationship were so severe that swift action needed to be taken.

Hopefully, you will not encounter such circumstances. However, if you are unlucky enough to do so, then bear in mind that it is rare for a tribunal to find that it is acceptable to dispense with any sort of formal process. Although the employer may have been right in this case that the relationship was beyond repair, a tribunal will usually want to see that every effort has been made to make it right. For example, in this case, the employer could have explained the reasons why it was considering dismissal and asked Mrs Gallacher to a formal meeting to discuss these. This would have given Mrs Gallacher the opportunity to put her side across. Mrs Gallacher could also have been given the opportunity to appeal. It is unlikely that the appeal process would have delayed matters or caused any further loss of trade, as Mrs Gallacher would have left the business upon her initial dismissal.

The importance of trying all angles before dismissal was emphasised in *Phoenix House Ltd v Stockman [2016] IRLR 848*. The EAT said that for an employer to fairly dismiss for 'some other substantial reason', it is not enough that two employees are not getting on. The relationship in question must be at the point of no return, with no reasonable prospect of the employees ever being able to work together again. One way of making sure you have tried everything to make a relationship work is to turn to mediation, which is covered later in this book.

Conflicting rights and beliefs

Another tricky form of conflict in the workplace is where an employee holds beliefs or expresses views that are at odds with the beliefs or protected characteristics of other staff. These particularly emotive situations have rapidly shot up employers' lists of priorities. Not only because we live in an opinionated era of social media and the Twittersphere but also due to courts and tribunals increasingly finding that employees' beliefs are brought within the scope of a 'protected characteristic'. This wide interpretation has covered a broad spectrum of modern trends and popular movements, such as protecting the belief in mankind's obligation to mitigate climate change, ethical veganism and Scottish independence.

One of the most high-profile decisions to date was made in 2021 by the EAT in *Forstater v CGD Europe [2021] IRLR 706*. The EAT held that the gender-critical belief that biological sex cannot be changed did fall within the scope of a 'philosophical belief' and merited the protection of the *Equality Act 2010*. This meant that Ms Forstater could challenge the non-renewal of her contract (due to her allegedly offensive and 'transphobic' remarks) as discrimination on grounds of her protected philosophical belief.

The *Forstater* decision confirms that the definition of a philosophical belief worthy of protection is potentially very wide. The test for whether a belief is protected is that it must:

- Be genuinely held

- Not simply be an opinion or viewpoint based on the present state of information available

- Concern a weighty and substantial aspect of human life and behaviour

- Attain a certain level of cogency, seriousness, cohesion and importance

- Be worthy of respect in a democratic society, not be incompatible with human dignity and not be in conflict with the fundamental rights of others

This was set out by the tribunal in *Grainger plc and others v Nicholson [2010] 2 All E.R. 253*.

It is worth bearing this test in mind when conflict erupts. For example, if you have an employee who is an avid anti-vaxxer, whose lack of Covid-19 vaccination is causing some distress to a disabled member of staff who is critically vulnerable, how would you manage this dispute? We already know that the disabled member of staff is protected from discrimination. However, what about the anti-vaxxer? Maybe they are too. It is important to consider how to ensure fair treatment of both parties during conflict but suffice it to say these situations require careful handling and management, particularly as the courts have made clear that a wide spectrum of beliefs is worthy of protection and only those at the most extreme – for example, Nazism –

will fall outside it. This is important to remember, and where the beliefs of an employee clash with those of a colleague, try not to make any assessment as to which belief is more important. Even the courts themselves have steered away from doing this.

CHAPTER 2
The impact of conflict on staff

The causes of conflict are wide, but nevertheless, their impact is much the same. The performance and productivity of individual employees, teams and, therefore, the whole company suffers, as do attendance levels and staff turnover, with stress and anxiety being the main culprits. In fact, Acas in its 'Estimating the costs of workplace conflict' report estimates that close to 10 million people per year experience conflict at work. Of these, over half suffer stress, anxiety or depression as a result, which leads to absences, resignations and dismissals. As well as the personal impact on the staff and their teams, this has a financial impact. Acas estimates that conflict-related sickness absence costs employers £2.2 billion each year and that employers' spending on employee turnover as a result of conflict (including recruiting and training replacement staff) is close to £15 billion.

Given this, it is well worth taking the time to manage the impact of conflict on the well-being of staff. In particular, employers should look out for the telltale signs that an employee is suffering from difficulties with their mental health. Acas in its 'Dealing with stress in the workplace' guidance (archived) lists the following as common symptoms of stress:

- Changes in behaviour, mood or interaction with colleagues

- Changes in the standard of work

- Changes in focus on tasks

- Appearing tired, anxious or withdrawn, and less interested in tasks previously enjoyed

- Changes in appetite

- Increase in smoking and consumption of alcohol

- Increase in sickness absences

- Arriving late at work

A manager who believes a team member is displaying such symptoms and may be experiencing mental health difficulties should not delay in approaching the employee about this. The manager should arrange a meeting in private with the employee to discuss how they are feeling and what may lie behind the changes. If the employee's concerns are work related, then the manager should take steps to support the employee, such as changing reporting lines (if it is a management problem) or reducing or reallocating work. If it is a particular conflict that is causing or contributing to the employee's concerns, then this is an excellent reason to make (even greater) efforts to resolve the conflict.

Another reason for tackling the impact of conflict on mental health is that not doing so can lead to court or tribunal claims, including for disability discrimination (if an employee suffers from a long-term mental health condition) and constructive unfair dismissal. If the impact of the conflict on an employee's mental health is sufficiently serious, it can also lead to a personal injury claim. This is because under health and safety legislation an employer has a duty to provide a safe place and system of work that should ensure the health, safety and welfare of its employees (so far as is reasonably practicable). If an employee considers that the employer has breached this duty by allowing or enabling the conflict and that they have suffered an injury to their mental health as a result, they can bring a claim for personal injury in court. However, to do so, the employee's mental health condition must be a clinically diagnosed psychiatric illness.

Given this potential for legal liability, it is important for the employer to understand how best to support the employee. If the employee will open up to their manager about how they are feeling and what can be done, then that is a great bonus. However, it is not always easy to persuade an employee to do so. In this circumstance, it may be preferable to tap into external sources of assistance. For example, if the employer provides an Employee Assistance Programme (EAP), the employee should be told or reminded of it and encouraged to access it. EAPs are schemes funded by employers that enable employees to access independent, professional support on a confidential basis. This support should help employees deal with any personal or work-related problems (including their feelings and perception about work-related conflict) that may be impacting their performance at work. The support made available will vary between EAP providers but often includes a 24/7 helpline, counselling services, legal information and financial advice.

Importantly, although EAPs are not 'a panacea by which employers can discharge their duty of care in all cases' (according to the Court of Appeal in *Intel Corporation (UK) Ltd v Daw [2007] IRLR 355)*, their use has been encouraged by courts and tribunals and can help in the employer's defence of claims. However, in all but the most serious of cases, the facts and content of an employee's discussions with an EAP remain confidential. This means that an EAP is not particularly helpful for the employer's purposes of actively managing the conflict or for understanding its impact on the employee's mental health.

For these purposes, using the services of an occupational health provider is recommended, particularly given their expertise in assessing the way in which employees' health can be impacted by the working environment and working practices.

In this case, an employer can take the initiative and request that the employee attend a consultation with an occupational health practitioner. The employer will usually pay for this, but it is well worth the money if it results in a detailed and reliable report on the employee's condition and steps the employer can take to support them. This can help the employer ensure that it complies with its duty to provide a safe place and system of work and to make the appropriate reasonable adjustments to the workplace if the employee is disabled.

A further advantage of using an occupational health provider in these circumstances is that they are well placed to ask the employee tricky questions about how work (or their personal life) is impacting their health – questions that managers can find difficult to ask and that many employees would prefer not to answer.

Not only does this help the employer provide a safe(r) workplace for the employee but it can also help clarify exactly how the employee considers the workplace conflict to be impacting their health and what the employee considers may resolve it (perhaps with some input from the occupational health practitioner). For example, the report may reveal a toxic relationship that the employee had not previously opened up about and re-frame the conflict as one involving bullying or harassment, in which case, making changes within the team or reporting lines may help to resolve the situation.

However, do bear in mind that employees should not be forced to attend an occupational health consultation if they do not wish to do so, even if there is a clause in their contract that requires it. It may be potentially justified to issue a disciplinary warning in these circumstances (as long as you follow a fair procedure), but this will not help to get a report (in the short term at least). Also, even if the employee does attend the consultation, as with all employer requests for medical reports, occupational health practitioners are bound by medical confidentiality. All information provided by the employee to the practitioner can only be given to the employer with the employee's informed consent. If an employee does not want the report to be disclosed to the employer, they can refuse to allow it. This may still leave an employer in the dark about how best to support the employee, in which case, it is even more important that resolving the conflict becomes a priority.

CHAPTER 3
Resolving conflict

One of the key findings in Acas's 'Estimating the costs of workplace conflict' report was that employers who put effort into effective and early resolution of conflict are rewarded both financially and in terms of reputation. So, how can employers resolve conflict at an early stage? The best option is to do so informally.

Informal conflict resolution

The most important step is to make sure managers spot and respond to problems. Also, they should get in touch with HR for assistance when needed. Indeed, where the culture in a workplace is to deal with conflict before matters come to a head, there tends to be regular dialogue between managers and HR. As many readers will have experienced, a brief pep talk before a manager handles a difficult conversation with a team member can save hours of time spent dealing with a formal grievance process.

It is very important that managers do not ignore issues and hope they will go away. The proverb that 'no news is good news' is, unfortunately, frequently misleading.

Often, employees do not take steps to raise an issue until the problem has really become entrenched. Good, consistent, objective and open communication between managers and their staff is really key to nipping conflict in the bud. It also gives employees a 'voice' and lets them be heard. This is particularly the case if the root of the conflict is based on a misunderstanding. For example, a conflict might be expressed as a performance issue, but there could be other tensions underneath, such as a relationship breakdown or resentment over not being promoted. One-to-one meetings with individual team members are great for this.

Once the manager has gained a clear understanding of the conflict and the different perspectives of the staff involved, it may be a good idea to bring the disputing employees together. The manager, or a member of the HR team, can then act as an objective facilitator to find common ground.

However, sometimes, this type of informal approach is not enough, particularly with less experienced managers or more serious issues. And sometimes, HR's profile is at stake and you just need to be seen to be dealing with conflict on a more formal basis.

That said, before resorting to a formal procedure, it may be appropriate to try another way of resolving the dispute, such as mediation.

Mediation

This is a type of alternative dispute resolution (ADR) that is conventionally understood to include four ways of resolving disputes: mediation, arbitration, negotiation and conciliation. The aim of all of these is to avoid litigation. Mediation is a particularly useful tool as it can be less formal and more flexible than other ADR methods. It is a voluntary and confidential process that can take place before, during or after a formal process. Mediation can be used in many different settings and to address many forms of conflict. However, this book focuses on workplace mediation. In other words, it focuses on mediation used to resolve any type of workplace conflict, such as resolving allegations of harassment or discrimination, performance management or a breakdown of trust.

Workplace mediation can take place remotely, by phone, at work or at a neutral venue. There has been a significant increase in 'virtual' mediation since the Covid-19 pandemic, and this can be particularly beneficial where relationships have broken down to such an extent that it is difficult for two (or more) people to be in the same room together. By carrying out the mediation online, the fact that the people are not physically sitting opposite each other can give them an increased sense of psychological security. Further, if the relationship has deteriorated to the extent that one party does not even want to set eyes on the other, then the camera can be turned off unless or until things improve. Virtual mediation can also be very useful when one of the employees is on sick leave and would find it hard to attend a mediation in person. In fact, without the ability to hold the mediation online, it may not be possible for it to take place at all. This would be unfortunate, as mediation can be a very useful tool to encourage someone on long-term sick leave to return to the workplace. Mediation is also a good way of ensuring communication with the absent employee and keeping them connected with the workplace whilst maintaining efforts to deal with any unresolved conflict. This is particularly useful where the employee's illness is linked to work, such as workplace stress or dysfunctional relationships.

Another advantage of workplace mediation is that it can all take place in-house by using trained internal mediators (whether HR or other employees) with no need for external assistance. This means that a need for mediation can be swiftly met without having to spend time (or money) trying to find an external mediator who is available (and good). Also, internal mediators are likely to know the business very well and can place the conflict in context from the start. That said, setting up an internal mediator scheme can get expensive, so small or medium-sized companies that will only need to use a mediator occasionally may prefer to use an external mediator, particularly as mediators are expected to act impartially (or at least be perceived to) and this can get difficult in a smaller company where everyone knows each other. Also, in a smaller company where the need for mediation is occasional, an internal mediator may not get sufficient opportunity to practice and hone their skills, in which case, using an external mediator instead of, or to work alongside, the internal mediator is likely to be the preferred option.

One way to try to ensure that mediation is used in the best and most appropriate way is to build it into your procedures, for example, by specifying when and how your formal processes may be paused or shelved in order to explore mediation and what type of mediator is appropriate in each situation. However, if incorporating mediation into your policies, do remember that it is voluntary. If one or more parties involved do not want to mediate, or it is not appropriate, then you will need to find another solution.

One of the main benefits of mediation is that there does not need to be a 'winner' and a 'loser', which makes for a better chance of mending a broken relationship. For this reason, it is particularly encouraged by Acas and the CIPD, both of which would like to see more widespread use of mediation to resolve conflict.

If you are a member of the HR Inner Circle (see the back of this book for more information), you can access a one-hour talk by Antony Sendall of www.mediationrescue.co.uk about the benefits of workplace mediation and how it works. Have a look at the recordings of the HR Inner Circle Annual Conference 2023 – you'll find it there.

Acas

The foreword to the Acas Code of Practice on disciplinary and grievance procedures (the Acas Code) contains a strong recommendation that mediation be considered. The value is that, if done well, mediation offers a safe and confidential space for those involved to find their own answers, which then have a greater chance of lasting.

The Acas website has information on how it can support employers with mediation. It says that it can:

- Provide external mediators

- Advise employers on introducing mediation

- Train staff in mediation

However, Acas cannot provide mediation to an employer that is involved in early conciliation or if a tribunal claim has been brought against the employer by one of its employees.

The benefit of using an external Acas mediator is that they are independent and impartial. Indeed, Acas says that in 2019-2020, 76% of Acas-led mediations were fully or partially resolved. However, if you prefer internal mediation, Acas can help with this also. The Acas 'Mediation at work' guide says that if employers want to set up an internal mediation scheme, one of the first steps to take is to select employees to act as internal mediators. To do so, employers can ask employees to volunteer and managers to nominate employees.

If employees do volunteer, Acas suggests that it is a good idea to set minimum standards that the volunteers should meet, such as having an understanding of conflict management. This will help make sure that only those who meet certain criteria apply and that there are not too many applications to review. Acas recommends that a diverse range of employees be selected to act as mediators. This will help employers to match mediators to parties more easily and make sure that mediators are impartial.

Once staff have been selected to act as mediators, employers should:

- Make sure mediation responsibilities are included in their job descriptions

- Make sure they understand their role and how it fits in with their organisation's policies and procedures

- Give employees time off for mediation

- Train them in mediation techniques

To help with this training, Acas offers in-person or remote accredited mediation training called the Certificate in Internal Workplace Mediation (CIWM). Acas says that its training gives staff the skills and knowledge they need to effectively mediate in their own workplace. It does so through role play and discussions focused on:

- What causes conflict at work

- How to identify issues before they become bigger problems

- When and how to take action

- What to do in difficult situations

- How to encourage people to take part in mediation

Acas suggests piloting any internal mediation scheme first to see if it works. Then, if it's successful, it can be expanded. Acas also recommends that a person or team is made responsible for overseeing mediation arrangements, for example, telling potential parties about the mediation process and keeping statistics to evaluate the scheme.

However, Acas is only one of a number of organisations that can provide training for internal mediators or supply external mediators. If you are interested in finding a mediator, The Civil Mediation Council has a 'Find a Mediator' search function on its website that could help.

Process

Whichever model or mediator you choose, there are some basic common stages in the mediation process.

1. **One-to-one meeting:** The mediator will usually first meet each party separately. This is the mediator's opportunity to listen to each party's perspective, understand their experiences of the dispute and what they want to get from the process and answer any questions they may have.

2. **Joint meeting:** At this meeting, the parties will come together and the mediator will facilitate a discussion. Usually, there is some uninterrupted time at the start of the session for each party to take turns to speak and, importantly, to listen. This is a crucial part of the process. The mediator's role is to encourage the parties to collaborate and help each party to understand the other party's point of view. This will help both parties to identify the issues on which they can more easily find common ground and those which may be tougher to resolve. The parties can then focus on these and the mediator can help them look forward (rather than dwelling on past differences) towards a mutually acceptable solution. This can be agreed in writing or just verbally.

3. **Follow up:** Many models of mediation will have a follow-up stage; this may be a few weeks later, and it is a chance to check how any agreements are working.

In particularly difficult cases where there is a high level of tension or hostility, the parties need not come face to face. The mediator can act as a go-between, seeking clarification of the respective positions, steering the conversations and encouraging the parties to consider different perspectives and options. Mediation is not about hearing evidence and establishing who is wrong or right. Its only focus is to find a fair and workable solution that allows both parties to move on. This is a good reason for turning to mediation even before starting a formal procedure. Even though such procedures are internal, they can become adversarial and focus on hearing evidence at an early stage, which can lead to employees taking entrenched and stubborn positions.

For example, where two senior people in a business simply cannot work together, rather than letting it get to the stage where you need to consider dismissing one of the parties, a mediator could help them see the other's point of view and find a way of working together. Also, even if one or both parties refuse mediation and you do go on to dismiss, showing that you made attempts to have the conflict mediated should stand you in good stead in defending any unfair dismissal claim. This is because, as covered in Chapter 1, before dismissing for 'some other substantial reason', an employer must reasonably conclude the relationship cannot be repaired.

Solutions

Another real positive about mediation is the flexibility in solutions. The mediation can result in an entirely bespoke arrangement that incorporates all sorts of things that a more formal decision or resolution wouldn't encompass. For example, agreeing some sort of change to the employee's terms and conditions, such as a change in working hours, a move to a new team or additional training. It could even result in a wholesale change to the working relationship, for example, agreeing the end of an employment contract but replacing it with a new relationship, such as the employer becoming a client of the ex-employee's consultancy.

When not to use mediation

Unfortunately, mediation is not always appropriate. Acas has identified certain situations in which this is likely to be the case:

- A decision about right or wrong is needed (for example, where possible criminal activity is involved).

- The employee is bringing a discrimination or harassment case and wants to have it investigated.

- The employee is vulnerable or has learning or mental health difficulties that would impair their ability to make an informed choice.

- The parties do not have the power to settle the issue.

- One party is stubborn or not committed, and mediation would only raise unrealistic expectations of a positive outcome.

If one or more of these apply, or if the mediation needs to be abandoned – for example, if serious allegations are made part way through – then you are likely to need to use a formal procedure, such as the grievance procedure.

Formal procedures

Although it may seem disappointing to need to resort to a formal procedure, it can be the most appropriate choice, despite all the time, effort and aggravation involved. In fact, if a dispute involves allegations of serious discrimination or harassment, you should actively encourage the alleged victim to pursue the formal route, whether this is set out in your grievance, dignity at work or bullying and harassment policies or otherwise. You will want to investigate to get to the bottom of the allegations and will need to do so if you want to take disciplinary action against the alleged aggressor.

Grievance procedure

If an employee so chooses, they have the right to pursue their grievance through the formal process. It is implied into all contracts of employment that an employer will reasonably and promptly afford employees the opportunity to have their grievances addressed. A failure to follow or comply with the procedure may well amount to a serious breach of the implied duty of trust and confidence. This would allow the employee to resign and claim constructive unfair dismissal (if they have the required two years' service).

The importance of complying with the grievance process is also compounded by the penalty awarded for failure to comply with the Acas Code, which adds an extra 25% to any subsequent tribunal award. Therefore, if you are in any doubt about how an employee wants their concerns resolved, do clarify with them whether they wish to pursue the formal grievance procedure.

Also, remember that the grievance procedure (or any other procedure that you use to deal with the complaint) needs to comply with the requirements of the Acas Code. Interestingly though, if the grievance is raised on behalf of two or more people, the Acas Code does not apply. The Acas Code says that these 'collective' grievances should be handled in accordance with the employer's collective grievance process if it has one. However, this may be set to change, as in October 2020, the Government said it will work with Acas to expand the Acas Code to provide practical guidance for such collective grievances (*Labour Market Enforcement Strategy 2019 to 2020: government response*).

Another reason that it is very important to deal correctly with a grievance is that if it all goes wrong, this in itself could land you with a discrimination claim, a constructive dismissal claim or both. This was highlighted in *Martin v Parkam Foods Ltd [2006] ET/1800241/06*. Mr Martin, an openly gay man, was the subject of graffiti and offensive remarks. He complained and the company removed his name from beside the graffiti drawing, although the drawing itself remained. When his name reappeared next to the drawing, Mr Martin made a further complaint. As a result, notices were put up warning staff against drawing graffiti but without mention of homophobia. When Mr Martin raised this, he was told that there was little that could be done and that it was probably not possible to discover who was responsible. Mr Martin resigned, raised a grievance and brought claims for constructive dismissal and direct discrimination, harassment and victimisation on the grounds of sexual orientation. The tribunal upheld his claims, criticised the employer's level of investigation and made several comments about the inadequate way the employer had dealt with homophobia in its workplace. The tribunal found that the employer would have put more effort into dealing with Mr Martin's grievance if it had not related to homophobia and that the employer had an in-built prejudice, even if it did not recognise this itself.

So how do you deal correctly with a grievance? Firstly, it is important to say that the Acas guidance on discipline and grievances at work advises that employers deal with grievances involving fellow employees carefully. Conversations should be handled in a way that is sensitive to the circumstances and the needs of the individuals concerned. It is important not to make assumptions at the outset about the facts of the case. Remember that both the accused and the accuser have rights and there is still a duty of trust and confidence owed to the accused. Meetings with the accused should be carried out with an open mind and should not turn into disciplinary hearings.

Meeting

In terms of the process, it is much the same as usual. The first step is likely to be to invite the complainant to a formal grievance meeting to discuss the complaint. You may already have a good idea of what the concerns are, having clarified these at an earlier stage, but it is worth doing so again, particularly as at this stage, the employee has the right to be accompanied and may give some more thought to the issues as they are being formally pursued.

The aim of the grievance meeting at this initial stage is to obtain as much detail about the relevant facts and circumstances as reasonably possible. It is also an opportunity to clarify the nub of the matter, particularly if the written grievance rambles or reads more like *War and Peace*. Once this is done, the meeting can be adjourned so an investigation can take place.

Investigation

In respect of who investigates, the roles of grievance investigator and decision-maker may be combined.

In fact, matters raised in a grievance may be resolved more satisfactorily if the person hearing the grievance also investigates the issues. Given this, and particularly if it is a sensitive, complex dispute, such as a conflict between employees with competing protected characteristics or beliefs, it is best to involve someone more experienced or senior who has been trained in discrimination law and has experience carrying out investigations and chairing hearings.

It is also important that the investigator is impartial and that their appointment will not raise any conflicts of interest. For a small employer, where all senior management may already have been involved and said their piece, it may be appropriate to hire an external consultant. However, the Acas guidance advises that any decision to do so should be made after balancing 'the needs for fairness against a cost-effective and efficient investigation', which roughly translates as 'don't spend a fortune appointing externally unless you really have to'.

The usual rules apply for carrying out an investigation. The investigator should look into both sides of the conflict and establish all the facts, including those that make difficult reading for the employer. However, when dealing with conflict between employees, there are some special considerations. It is particularly important to make sure everything is kept confidential. Don't assume that witnesses involved in the investigation will instinctively keep the details to themselves. The need for confidentiality should be spelt out in no uncertain terms.

Careful consideration should also be given to the working relationship between the employees whilst the investigation is ongoing. For example, to prevent any bullying or harassment being repeated, one of the parties could be temporarily redeployed, be allowed to work permanently from home or have their reporting line changed. However, where such measures are used, the employees affected should be treated fairly by the employer. For example, the employer should only transfer an employee to a job of similar status. As a last resort, suspension on full pay could be considered. It does need to be strictly necessary and not just the easiest or 'knee-jerk' reaction. It should be made clear to the suspended employee that it is not a disciplinary action. How you handle these measures and decide who they apply to can be difficult. Be careful, as you do not want anybody to feel they are being victimised for raising a concern. Discuss your concerns and potential measures with the employees before you identify the most appropriate action. For example, the decision about who to move could depend on factors such as workload or whose role can more easily be performed from another site or from home.

The final stage of the investigation, particularly for complex and serious allegations, is for the investigator to put together an investigation report. This should contain details of what the grievance is, the steps taken in the investigation, the most important evidence, the investigator's conclusions and any recommendations. Make sure any recommendations are limited to suggesting further action and do not prejudge the outcome of the grievance. For example, it is fine to suggest changes to one of the employer's policies or procedures, but it is not acceptable to recommend disciplinary action is taken against the accused.

Once the investigation is complete, a grievance meeting should be set up or reconvened before any decision is taken. The complainant should be presented with any relevant reports and/or witness and documentary evidence a reasonable period before the meeting so they have enough time to consider them. At the reconvened meeting, the employee should be given the opportunity to comment on any evidence.

Outcome

The final stage is for the chair of the hearing to make their decision and to recommend any next steps and appropriate action. The type of action will depend on the nature of the grievance, but usually, when the complaint relates to conflict, the aim will be to stop it happening again. So, examples in this situation could include moving employees, providing training or taking disciplinary action.

The employee who raised the grievance should be informed in writing of whether it is upheld, what actions are recommended and their right of appeal. You could, in addition, hold a meeting with the employee. If the grievance is not upheld, then provide a careful explanation of the reasons for that decision. It is also important to feed back to any employees implicated in the grievance on any aspects of the decision that affect them and why.

If the outcome of the grievance is that disciplinary action should be taken against an employee, it is important that the usual disciplinary process is followed and any sanction is only decided after a disciplinary hearing.

An HR Inner Circle member once dealt with a situation with where an employee appealed a grievance outcome because they had not been told whether the other employee (who was the subject of the grievance) was disciplined as a result. The aggrieved employee assumed that because the other employee was still in employment, no action had been taken by the employer. Some very delicate conversations had to take place to reassure them that the process had been satisfactorily handled without breaching confidentiality for the other party.

If the conflict is still not resolved, there are still options to try to avoid litigation. As mentioned, mediation is a very good way of dealing with most forms of conflict. It is also particularly good for rebuilding relationships after the completion of a formal process, such as the grievance procedure. So, you could get an external mediator in (or back in) or use one of your own and try to work on repairing some of the damage caused by the conflict. You could maybe use the recommendations in the grievance decision as a focus.

Settlement

If one of the parties remains disgruntled to the extent that they may bring a claim in the employment tribunal, you may want to take steps to settle the issue before that happens. Or, even if a claim is not yet on the cards but you consider that it would be better for business if the employee exits the business, a 'settlement agreement' could be the answer. This is a legally binding contract between employer and employee that settles claims that the employee may have against their employer in return for money and/or other benefits.

Settlement can be a great way of resolving conflict in a way that keeps everyone happy, but not always, so tread carefully. Once you raise the issue of settlement with an employee, there is rarely any going back, particularly if you want to negotiate an employee's exit. The mere mention of settlement could be viewed as offensive by the employee and as an ill-disguised attempt to force them to resign. It could end up in a messy constructive dismissal or discrimination claim.

Also bear in mind that before entering into a settlement agreement, the employee will need to take independent advice on its terms. If you think that sending the employee to get such advice would open a Pandora's box of troubles that would negate any benefits to settlement (or cost too much), then it may be wise to pursue another way of resolving the conflict.

If you decide that settlement is worth pursuing, then tread carefully and take the time to plan the process before approaching the employee. It is recommended that you take advice from a legal professional to help you with this.

Keeping it confidential – without prejudice and protected conversations

Central to any settlement plan is how best to keep the settlement discussions 'off the record' so that they cannot later come back to bite you if negotiations fail and you end up at tribunal. In other words, remember to use the 'without prejudice' or 'protected conversation' rules that should help protect your settlement discussions (whether written or verbal) from being repeated in front of a judge.

To gain the benefit of 'without prejudice' protection, your settlement discussions need to be genuinely aimed at resolving an existing dispute with the employee. This means the discussions need to take place in the spirit of compromise. In other words, they should involve some offer or concession(s) to help pave the way towards compromise and eventual settlement. If you use fraudulent means of persuading the employee to settle or otherwise exert 'undue influence' or some other 'unambiguous impropriety', like blackmail or perjury, the 'without prejudice' protection will be lost.

Importantly, for an actual or potential dispute to exist, there should at least be signs that the employee is aggrieved to the extent that they are considering bringing a claim or might reasonably have done so. This will be straightforward if an employee has said that they intend to bring, or have brought, a tribunal claim. However, it may not always be quite as obvious. So, if you are not yet at the stage where an employee has brought a claim, you should look at whether there are signs they are considering this. For example, a grievance in itself does not necessarily amount to an existing dispute as it may be settled to an employee's satisfaction, in which case there's no longer an argument or dispute. However, where the employer does not (or does not intend to) uphold the grievance, there may well be a dispute. Also, a breakdown in relationships due to the conflict – for example, between an employee and their manager when dealing with performance management – may evidence an existing dispute.

However, particularly in situations where you have decided that the employee is no longer a good fit for the business, a dispute may well not exist (yet). In this situation, your best bet is likely to be to take the 'protected conversation' route. This is set out under section 111A of the *Employment Rights Act 1996* and is designed to keep any 'pre-termination' conversations you have with an employee (where there's no actual dispute) confidential. In other words, conversations where you make an offer to the employee and discuss termination on agreed terms will be inadmissible if the employee brings an unfair dismissal claim.

That said, take care if the situation involving the employee is complex and there are other factors at play that mean the employee could bring additional claims. Section 111A of the *Employment Rights Act 1996* does not apply in every 'no dispute' situation. Where there is an automatically unfair reason for dismissal – for example, asserting a statutory right, whistleblowing or trade union membership – your conversations will not be protected and you will not be able to keep them confidential. The protection also will not apply in a whole raft of other potential claims, including discrimination, breach of contract and wrongful dismissal. Further, section 111A of the *Employment Rights Act 1996* will not apply where there has been 'improper behaviour'. This is similar to 'without prejudice' but with a slightly lower threshold. The Acas Code lists examples as:

- Harassment, bullying and intimidation through offensive words and aggressive behaviour.

- Physical assault (actual or threatened) and other criminal behaviour.

- Victimisation.

- Discrimination.

- Putting undue pressure on a party. This includes telling an employee, before the disciplinary process has started, that if they don't agree to a settlement proposal, they'll be dismissed. It also includes not giving the employee enough time to consider a proposed settlement.

Negotiating the agreement

As part of your settlement plan, you need to decide your preferred medium for conducting the negotiations. Doing so in person is usually best. A settlement process conducted by letter, email or text is generally a bad idea as it does not set the right tone and can easily lead to misunderstandings.

It is recommended (certainly at the outset) that you meet with the employee face to face. It is good practice and it can be helpful to allow the employee to bring a work colleague or trade union representative along too. The employee doesn't have a legal right to this, but it can be useful (for both parties) to have someone else there.

At the meeting, it is important that you are clear about why you have asked to meet with the employee and what you hope to get out of your discussions. This will be easy to explain in circumstances where the employee has already declared their intention to bring a claim. If they have not, you may need to put more thought into how you approach the conversation. Probably the best way to start is to explain your concerns about the employee's performance, conduct or other conflict situation. Then let them know about the 'without prejudice' or 'protected conversation' rules and explain that the discussions you are having will probably be inadmissible at a tribunal if it comes to that. Try to get them to consent to the conversations remaining confidential and to buy into the aim of avoiding litigation. That will help keep your conversations away from a judge.

Move on to explaining that you propose a settlement and, if you wish them to leave the business, how that will be managed. Present it as an offer or opportunity for the employee to consider, not as a done deal that you wish to pressure them into taking.

Make clear that any formal procedures you may currently be following are unaffected by the discussions. In other words, you will continue to deal with any grievance, disciplinary or performance management procedure (or other method of dealing with the conflict) in the usual way and 'on the record'. This is important. It makes clear to the employee that not only do they still have other options but also that you do too. In other words, it shows that you are not desperate to settle their (prospective) claim at all costs. Furthermore, if settlement negotiations break down, at least you will have another route to follow.

Indeed, if the employee tells you at this first meeting that they are not interested in settlement, then it may be best to move on and focus on the 'on the record' process instead. You cannot force them into it.

If the employee seems interested in settlement, the next step is to clarify what you are offering and get written terms drawn up and provided to the employee. Think widely about these terms and outside of just the amount of cash on offer. While money is often the key driver for an employee to agree to a settlement, other things might help get the deal over the line. For example, if possible, you could agree to a positive reference or wording for announcing their departure, or even an offer of consultancy work in the future. If they are not exiting the business, then you could agree to move them to a different location or to work under a different line manager.

A member of the HR Inner Circle suggests that where an employee wants more money than the employer is prepared to offer, the employer can suggest that a reference is effectively worth the annual salary of their next job, as without a reference, there may well be no offer of employment. Bear in mind, though, that if the employee is alleging any form of discrimination, this may be seen as unlawful victimisation (i.e., as a threat to withhold a favourable reference unless the employee agrees not to pursue their discrimination claim).

Remember that for these terms to be binding, you will need to enter a settlement agreement with the employee. If you are being advised by a lawyer on this (which is a very good idea at this stage), then they will be able to draft this for you. The terms of the agreement generally provide for a severance payment (and any other benefits or 'sweeteners') to be provided by the employer in return for an employee's agreement not to pursue any claims in a tribunal or court. The terms of the agreement and the surrounding circumstances of the dispute are usually required to be kept confidential.

An HR Inner Circle member emphasises the importance of a well-drafted letter outlining the terms of the agreement, and the basis or conditions upon which it has been offered. It is easy to forget that the employee is seeing or hearing the settlement terms for the first time, likely with no prior experience of the process and certainly with no prior view of the planning or approach. Providing the employee with a clearly thought through letter, as opposed to only a legal agreement document on its own, can also help their chosen advisor understand the context in which the offer is being given. This, in turn, can help the advisor to give on-point advice and support to the employee, making for smoother, more amicable negotiations.

As mentioned earlier, the employee needs to take independent advice on the terms of the agreement. Give them reasonable time to consider the terms and take advice. The Acas Code of Practice on settlement agreements says to allow at least 10 calendar days, but this will depend on the situation. The employee will most often take this advice from a qualified lawyer, but it could also be a trade union rep or an advice worker (from an advice centre) if they are certified as competent to do so. It is the employer who generally pays for this advice, which is generally in the range of £350 to £800 plus VAT. However, this cost and the sum paid in settlement are usually well worth it if they avoid the expense (and emotional drain) of fighting a tribunal claim.

Conciliation

Conciliation is similar to mediation in that it is voluntary, but it is normally used in the later stages of a dispute when the employee is preparing to make or has made a tribunal claim.

The best-known form of conciliation is the Acas early conciliation procedure. Its purpose is to encourage early settlement and avoid tribunal proceedings. It applies to most forms of tribunal claims and anyone who wants to bring such a claim must first contact Acas to allow them to attempt to conciliate a settlement. The process 'stops the clock' in the limitation period so that settlement negotiations don't disadvantage the employee in terms of the timescales for bringing a claim. There are four main parts to the process:

1. The employee kick-starts the process by contacting Acas by phone, email or post.

2. Acas then contacts the employee to discuss the claim. If the employee wants to conciliate, the Acas officer will gather information about the

claim. If the employee does not want to conciliate, Acas will issue what's called an EC certificate.

3. If the employee is willing to conciliate, Acas will contact the employer. If Acas cannot contact the employer after reasonable attempts, or if the employer does not want to conciliate, Acas will issue an EC certificate.

4. If both parties agree to conciliate, they will have a period of six weeks to negotiate a settlement. If no settlement is reached once this period ends, Acas will issue an EC certificate. Obviously, if matters are settled, then things come to a natural end without the need for an EC certificate.

This early conciliation process can be a very effective (and free!) way of settling a dispute. It provides an independent and impartial Acas officer who will:

• Explain the conciliation process

• Discuss the issues with both sides

• Give an overview of the law

• Discuss how tribunals have considered cases similar to yours

• Help both sides explore the strengths and weaknesses of the case

• Discuss possible options without making any recommendations

- Remain independent of the dispute – they will not take sides or tell you what to do

- Outline the tribunal process

This can be a particularly useful process when dealing with employees who have little or no knowledge of employment law or the tribunal process. It can focus the mind on what bringing a claim entails and its potential financial (and emotional) costs. However, there are downsides. The employee or employer can refuse to engage and the extent to which the Acas officer really gets to grips with the issues involved does vary. On occasion, it can appear that the officer is little more than a messenger.

If the process is a success and you reach an agreement, Acas will record what is agreed in a settlement form called a COT3. Once both parties agree to it (even if it is not yet signed), it is legally binding and, similar to a settlement agreement, it settles the claim that has been brought or any other potential claims arising out of the same circumstances. However, unlike a settlement agreement, it does not require the employee to take independent legal advice on its terms in order for it to be valid. Also, a COT3 can only be used with Acas's involvement and only once an employee has decided to bring a claim, whereas a settlement agreement can also be used in circumstances where a claim is not contemplated and a dispute has not even arisen, for example, to bring an employee's contract of employment to an end on agreed terms.

Acas can also help with 'collective conciliation'. This is where there is a dispute between an employer and a group of employees. Its process is similar to that followed in workplace mediation. Acas will provide an independent and impartial conciliator who will meet with the parties individually and together to try to find common ground to help them arrive at a solution. Collective conciliation is particularly helpful in resolving disputes about:

- Annual pay reviews

- Other pay issues

- Contract terms and conditions

- Changes in working practices

- Discipline and dismissal, if an employee representative or a group of people are involved

- Redundancy consultation and redundancy selection

- Trade union recognition

Arbitration

Arbitration involves a private agreement to resolve disputes outside of tribunal litigation but still in a judicial way. Similar to litigation, the parties need to attend a 'hearing' that takes place in front of a neutral decision-maker called an 'arbitrator', who is selected by both parties. The parties need to agree that the arbitrator's decision will be legally binding.

During the hearing, the arbitrator will listen as the parties present evidence, may ask questions of the parties and their witnesses and may ask for any further evidence that they consider relevant to deciding the claim. Sometime after arbitration, the arbitrator will make a decision about the case and will record their decision in writing. The decision is final and binding, and the parties can bring a claim against the other if they act in breach of it.

Arbitration is becoming more popular, and Acas offers a free arbitration scheme for individuals about unfair dismissal and flexible working claims. Acas also offers collective arbitration for disputes between an employer and a group of employees.

Judicial mediation

If it gets to the stage where an employee brings a tribunal claim, then 'judicial mediation' may be appropriate to resolve the dispute. It takes place after Acas early conciliation but before the claim has advanced too far along the tribunal process, and it takes the form of a private preliminary hearing in front of a trained employment judge. The role of the employment judge is not to make a decision on the merits of the claim but to remain neutral and to assist the parties in resolving their dispute between themselves. The process generally involves the judge acting as the go-between for the parties, having individual meetings with them separately and passing messages between them. This is different from 'workplace mediation' (which was explored earlier in this chapter) where joint meetings between both (or all) of the parties are more common.

The judicial mediation process generally takes one to two days and, if successful, the employee's claim will usually be settled by way of a settlement agreement or COT3 (if Acas is involved).

Unfortunately, if judicial mediation or any of the other forms of dispute resolution are not successful, the next stop is usually expensive tribunal proceedings.

CHAPTER 4
Preventing future conflict

For many reasons, including the financial cost and the emotional toll on all those involved, it is best to resolve conflict quickly and fairly. Even better, though, is to try to prevent such conflict in the first place. Although it is very unlikely that an employer will be able to eradicate conflict entirely – after all, it is dealing with people, not robots – there are steps the employer can all take to manage it. In particular, the employer can encourage and embed the principles of dignity and respect into the workplace culture. Not only should this help deal with conflicts based on discriminatory behaviour or views but also, as you are all no doubt highly aware, dignity and respect are very valid cornerstones for people management in general, whether or not staff have a protected characteristic or protected belief. The CIPD recommends that senior leaders take a visible lead on this and set the tone for appropriate behaviour. The CIPD also recommends that they should emphasise the importance of respect between employees at every level.

But of course, 'preventing future conflict' can be seen as 'trying to keep everyone happy' – an impossible task. When problems arise, they tend to have been simmering for some time and no book will give you the tools you need to prevent problems that are not apparent. One method that can work is to provide something that encourages staff to talk freely about changes they may like or even just talk together.

An HR Inner Circle member was concerned about two groups during the COVID-19 pandemic: those working at home and those attending a quiet office. A 'coffee morning' was set up to remotely connect home workers, and those still at the office were sent hampers of cakes or chocolate. The telling point was when a member of staff reported: "Moods were not good; people were on edge and the atmosphere in the office was very strained. Then the cakes arrived. Everyone stopped work and we all had coffee and chatted. We hadn't done that in weeks." The member believes this simple strategy forestalled an atmosphere that might otherwise have turned into a conflict situation.

That said, all employees have their part to play, as well as the right to have their voice heard as to how a culture might be improved. This upward flow of information could come via HR or managers or, in smaller organisations, there may be a communication channel straight to the top. The flip side of encouraging an open culture is that suggestions made and complaints raised need to be listened to and dealt with. Policies that deal with harassment or speaking up should be visible and brought to life, maybe by carrying out a staff survey to take a temperature check regarding how to prevent conflict, or making discussion about bullying, harassment or other conflict a topic for regular one-to-one meetings.

A member of the HR Inner Circle recommends pulse surveys as a good way to clarify any areas of concern. They also recommend working closely with unions on an informal basis or having a staff group that can help provide colleagues with the ability to raise concerns informally.

In designing new ways of working for a start-up, another HR Inner Circle member has approached this through embedding more adult-adult conversations into everyday work. This ranges from discussing 'pebbles' (small tensions, unresolved questions, etc.) at the start of any team meetings or one-to-one discussions to embedding a focus on responsibility and belief that the other person is able to reflect on and rectify any behaviour that is having an adverse impact on others. Treating people like adults as opposed to children and giving them the freedom to choose how to respond (in an adult way) enables more harmonious and constructive discussions in the workplace.

A third member of the HR Inner Circle recommends asking all employees (including new employees) to complete a well-being passport. This includes known triggers and times of year that need to be watched out for. The member also has a policy of always asking twice whether people are okay. Normally, on the first ask people say, "Yes, I'm fine", but on a second ask, you often get the real truth or something that helps you explore something further.

A particular area of preventing conflict where the government has got involved is sexual harassment, thanks largely to its recent high profile and the damage it can cause. The 2020 EHRC technical guidance, 'Preventing sexual harassment at work: a guide for employers', contains detailed advice for employers wanting to tackle sexual harassment, including that employers should have different policies to deal with sexual harassment and harassment related to other protected characteristics, or, alternatively, that employers should have one policy that clearly distinguishes between different forms of harassment. It also suggests the detail of what this policy should cover and that it is evaluated and reviewed annually. Finally, it suggests ways in which employers should be on the lookout for harassment, beyond responding to direct complaints, including an online or externally run telephone reporting system to allow staff to make complaints on either a named or anonymous basis.

The Government has also made it clear, in its July 2021 response to its consultation on sexual harassment in the workplace, that it will work with the EHRC to introduce a statutory code of practice. This is something that all employers will be legally bound to follow and will include a new duty requiring employers to 'take all reasonable steps' to prevent sexual harassment. This code may well be based on the EHRC technical guidance mentioned above – so it is worth having a look.

Central to preventing conflict is to have well-trained managers. They need to be given the skills and confidence to intervene at an early stage to nip disagreements in the bud before they become entrenched. Managers who build and maintain good working relationships with their team members will be able to pick up on any early warning signs that a low-level grumble might be on the cusp of erupting into a full-scale explosion and then have the confidence to step in and resolve it. So, training on how to deal with conflict and difficult conversations is key.

To try to avoid conflict connected to performance management, managers should be trained in how to set clear and realistic goals and to ensure their team members are not only aware of the expectations on them but also how to achieve them. As usual, good communication is key, and if an employee is underperforming, then it is important that the ways in which this is happening are explained clearly to them and to explore whether there are any workplace (or external) issues impacting their performance.

It is not only good communication between the manager and their team which is important. Clear communication should be encouraged at all levels, particularly now that hybrid and home working has really taken off. A lack of face-to-face communication in the daily workplace diet provides many opportunities for great slip-ups on the banana skins of quick email and social media messaging. As I'm sure you will have discussed with your staff, one-to-one meetings and actually talking still play a very important part in the workplace.

Also by
Daniel Barnett

Available on Amazon
or visit
go.danielbarnett.com/books

JOIN DANIEL EVERY SATURDAY EVENING AT
9PM WHEN HE PRESENTS THE ALL-NEW

LBC LEGAL HOUR

— OR CATCH UP VIA THE GLOBAL PLAYER,
AT bit.ly/lbclegalhour

SATURDAYS, 9PM

Dear HR Professional,

I take my hat off to you.

Having supported the HR community for so many years, I know It's a challenging job you do, sometimes under really difficult circumstances.

The tricky HR issues you have to handle must take up a tremendous amount of your time, your energy and your brain power. I bet it can be exhausting for you to work under that level of pressure.

Being An HR Professional In Today's Business Environment Is TOUGH!

Maintaining your high standards of professionalism must be a real struggle, especially when your efforts and expertise often go unappreciated.

I'll wager you have to make decisions on challenging HR situations you've sometimes never encountered before. Even if you're part of a team, it must sometimes feel like you're working in isolation.

With so much complexity and ambiguity, do you ever find you're not clear whether you're doing the right thing when there's so much to think about?

I expect it can be draining too. You've got to make tough decisions which may be unpopular.

The pressure's on you to ensure people are treated fairly while the business complies with its legal obligations.

It's a thankless task, especially if you've got grief coming at you from all sides.

Doubt can creep in too. Even though you're an extremely competent professional, you might even begin to question yourself... What if you've got it wrong?

You've got to cope with all that, whilst constantly having to convince any doubting stakeholders you're adding value to the business.

That pressure must take its toll on you.

You wouldn't be human if it didn't cause you tension, stress or even worse!

Being the caring professional you are, I bet you often take work home with you.

If You're Not Careful The Stress WILL Creep Up On You

And I don't just mean opening your laptop on your couch when everyone else is watching Eastenders.

We all know of families and relationships that come a poor second to the pressures and challenges faced at work.

Yours too..?

But does it have to be that way?

Should you feel the responsibility of the HR world is entirely on your shoulders and that you've got to bear that burden alone?

The answer is a firm no.

It doesn't have to be like that.

There Is An Answer To Help Make Your Work & Your Life Much Easier For You

There's a place you can get all the help, support, advice and encouragement you need to ease the constant pressure you have to bear.

It's called the
HR Inner Circle.

It will lift the burden you're carrying by giving you swift access to comprehensive resources and live practical guidance you can implement right away.

It's information I know will save you time, energy and effort.

It's a vibrant, active community of caring, like minded HR professionals willing to help you.

There are resources packed full of practical, actionable advice for you that's difficult to find anywhere else.

And it doesn't matter what you're working on.

Whether it be workforce engagement, attracting and keeping talent, diversity and inclusion or employee health and well being, you'll find support for all of that.

You're covered even if you're working on one of those tricky, sensitive, people problems you never see coming until they land squarely on your plate.

Timely Support To Make Your Job Easier, Can Be Rapidly Found In The HR Inner Circle

As a member of the HR Inner Circle, to get the support you want…

…just ask.

Your first port of call is the vibrant Facebook group, bursting at the seams with incredible HR professionals like you.

Just post your question and let it bubble and simmer in the collective genius of the group.

By the end of the day, you'll have at least 3-5 comments on your post, often more.

You'll get relevant, insightful and practical guidance that comes from the hard earned experience of your fellow members.

Often you'll get a response within a couple of hours. Sometimes you'll get an answer within minutes - even if it's late in the evening!

This highly active community never fails to astound me with just how willing they are to help fellow HR professionals like you.

They readily and generously share their hard earned knowledge and experience.

You Can Get Answers From <u>Real People</u> Quickly AND From Our Extensive Resource Library Too

> …really important for someone working on their own who needs to check things out, or just bounce a few ideas around.
>
> - Quentin Colborn
> Director, QC People Management Ltd

While you wait for a response from the Facebook group, you'll likely find answers in the resource-rich members' vault on our secure online portal as well.

It takes just 2 clicks and a quick keyword search using our Rapid Results Search Tool.

You'll instantly find precisely where your topic is covered in our extensive back catalogue of monthly magazines and audio seminars.

In under 30 seconds you can find exactly what you're after.

It's that quick and easy.

…And if you need a specific legal insight?

Then pose your question live to an expert employment lawyer in our monthly Q&A session.

It'll either be me or one of my prominent contemporaries. You'll get your answer immediately without having to pay any legal costs.

If you can't wait, you'll find where it's been answered before with a quick search of previous Q&A sessions.

Our clever index system means you can find a question, and in a single click get straight to the recorded answer.

But perhaps you need to dive deep and explore the different options open to you to solve a particularly tricky problem?

Then join one of our monthly HR Huddles. There you can run your specific situation past other HR professionals.

They'll offer their insights, share their experience and work WITH you to find a solution that works FOR you.

You'll find all of this in one convenient place - the HR Inner Circle.

It's Been A Labour Of Love Putting The HR Inner Circle Together So It Works For Professionals Like You

I've spent years practising law and have become recognised as one of the UK's leading employment law barristers. I've even got my own radio show!

But more importantly for you, I've also developed another skill.

It's bringing useful employment expertise AND practical experience together in a way that supports busy, overworked (and sometimes stressed) HR professionals like you.

Everything you're likely to need is **literally at your fingertips**.

This will save you **time, energy** and **effort**.

Being a member also means your business and clients will see you as even MORE INFORMED about the intricacies of employment law.

They'll marvel at how well you keep up to date when you're busy working so hard for them.

You'll be seen making quicker decisions and implementing effective solutions to accelerate the growth of the organisation.

You'll make impressive time and cost savings for the business.

And those tricky, off-piste situations you've never come across before..?

Well, nothing will faze you, because you're backed up by an HR support system second to none.

But more importantly, you'll feel that pressure gently ease off.

With the relief you'll feel knowing that such great help and guidance is just a few minutes, you'll wonder how you survived without it!

That's Why I'm Inviting You To Join And Reap The Many Rewards Of Membership

WWW.HRINNERCIRCLE.CO.UK

Here's what you get when you join the HR Inner Circle:

Benefit #1- you'll get unlimited access to the hugely popular HR Inner Circle Facebook Private Group

- Tap into the vast wealth of knowledge, experience, insight and wisdom of the top 0.5% of your profession at any time, day or night.

- In less than 5 minutes you can post ANY HR question and get insightful answers and suggestions in a couple of hours or less, from some of the best in your profession.

- Fast track your impact by discovering effective shortcuts and workarounds from HR people who've been "there" and done "it".

- Expand and deepen your network of like minded individuals, secure in the knowledge they're as dedicated and as ambitious as you.

- Increase your prestige with your colleagues and stakeholders by being part of such an exclusive and prominent HR community.

- Gain confidence in your judgment and decisions by using the highly responsive community as a sounding board for your ideas.

Benefit #2 - you'll receive 11 copies of the HR Inner Circular Magazine every year

- Enjoy that satisfying "THUD" on your door mat every month when the postman delivers your very own copy of the HR Inner Circular magazine.

- Quickly discover exactly what the law says about key issues affecting HR professionals around the UK like you.

- Get concise and practical guidance on how employment law applies to the challenging situations and circumstances you deal with every day.

- Avoid the mistakes of others by applying the lessons from the in depth analysis of real life case studies.

- Benefit from a legal deep dive by the UK's leading employment law barrister into a topical employment question posed by a fellow member (perhaps you!).

- Review a summary of recent important Facebook Group discussions worthy of sharing, that you may have missed.

- Explore a range of related and relevant topics useful for your practice and your broader professional development.

> The magazine is really informative, the Facebook group such a community, and I think exceptional value for money.
>
> - Lis Moore
> Head of Advisory & Support Services,
> Society of Local Council Clerks

Benefit #3 - Monthly Audio Seminars

- A 60 minute legal deep dive by me into an important subject relevant to you and your practice.

- Professionally recorded content recorded exclusively for the HR Inner Circle - you'll not find this information anywhere else.

- Carefully structured content that's easy to consume, understand and apply in your work as an HR professional.

- Episodes delivered every month so you can stay current on the latest issues affecting HR professionals.

- The convenience of listening to the recording online or downloading the mp3 for later enjoyment at a time suitable to your busy schedule (perfect for any commute).

Benefit #4 - you get an exclusive invite to a live online Q&A Session every fortnight, led by an expert employment lawyer

- Gain 60 minutes of live and direct access to the sharpest legal minds from my secret little black book of contacts.

- Get answers to your knottiest employment law questions, and solutions to your trickiest HR problems, from some of the brightest employment lawyers in the UK.

- Avoid having to pay the £300-£400 it would cost you to ask a lawyer your question outside of the HR Inner Circle.

- Benefit from valuable insights from the answers given to other members.

- If you can't attend live, watch the recording when it's convenient for you.

- Quickly access the recorded answer to any question asked in the session by simply clicking the question index for that session.

- Save time by downloading the session transcription to scan-read at a time suitable for you.

Benefit #5 - join a live Monthly Huddle with other HR Professionals to solve your most challenging HR problems

- Attend your very own mini-mastermind group of highly qualified, highly regarded and experienced fellow HR professionals to "group think" through an issue you're facing right now.

- Develop bespoke solutions to the unique problems and challenges you have to deal with in a safe, supportive and confidential environment.

- Feel safe knowing these online zoom calls are NOT recorded to respect the sensitivity of issues addressed and the privacy of those involved. [NOTE - a professional transcriber attends and takes written notes. An anonymised summary is then made available to the membership]

- Recent Huddle topics included changing employee benefits, mandatory vaccination, career breaks, sickness during disciplinaries, effective worker forums and hybrid working arrangements.

Benefit #6 - access our Templates & Resources Centre

- Gain immediate access to our library of the most popular and frequently used forms, assessments, agreements, checklists, letter templates, questionnaires and reports to help the busiest HR professionals save time and get things done quicker and easier.

- Download them as Word documents, so you can edit and personalise them to fit your business needs

- New templates added every single month

Benefit #7 - build your own Employment Law Library

- We send you several brand-new books on employment law several times each year

- Acquire your own physical library of concise, easy-to-read and fully updated textbooks

- Recent titles include Hiring Staff, Managing Sickness Absence, Spotting Malingering and Resolving Grievances

Benefit #8 - free Ticket to our Annual Conference

- The perfect opportunity to extend your personal network of fellow HR professionals.

- Meet up face to face with the people who've been supporting you in the Facebook Group and HR Huddles so you can deepen those connections even further.

- Gather key insights and takeaways to help you personally and professionally from some of the best speakers on the circuit. Previous speakers have covered motivation, dealing with difficult people, goal setting and productivity, decision making and social media marketing.

- Get instant access to recordings of all previous conferences so even if you can't attend in person, you can benefit from the event in your own time.

- Includes probably the best conference lunch you'll ever have - a bold claim I know, but we use outstanding caterers.

> It never ceases to amaze me the amount of time and effort people put into the Facebook group, sharing their experiences, advice, and sage words of wisdom.
>
> **- Emma Lister**
> HR Consultant, SME HR Services

Benefit #9 - your Personal Concierge will help you get the best out of your membership

- You get personal access to Nina who'll point you in the direction of exactly where to find what you need. She's supported hundreds of members over the 5 years she's been part of the team.

- Nina also works closely with the 11 back office staff that support the operation. In the extremely unlikely event she doesn't know where something is, she knows who will.

HOW MUCH DOES JOINING THE HR INNER CIRCLE COST?

There's no doubt in my mind the annual value of membership benefits is in the many thousands of pounds range.

But you're not going to pay anywhere near that.

Let me remind you of what that small monthly fee gives you every year

Access to the private Facebook Group	INCLUDED
HR Inner Circular Magazine subscription	INCLUDED
Monthly Audio Seminars	INCLUDED
Live Q&A sessions	INCLUDED
Monthly HR Huddles	INCLUDED
Templates & Resources Centre	INCLUDED
Employment Law Library	INCLUDED
Free ticket to the HR Inner Circle Annual Conference	INCLUDED
Your Personal Membership Concierge	INCLUDED

TOTAL PRICELESS

Another way of looking at your investment is this:

Because access to what you need is so quick…

Join today and that price is fixed for as long as you remain a member.   You'll always pay the same, even if we increase the price to new members (which we regularly do).

…it's like having your very own part time, legally trained, assistant HR Business Partner, just waiting to provide you with all the answers you need…

▶ WWW.HRINNERCIRCLE.CO.UK ◀

Plus, With Membership Of The HR Inner Circle, You'll Also Get These 4 Additional Resources For FREE!

Additional Resource #1 - Handling Awkward Conversations

A video case study masterclass you can share with managers to train them to handle awkward staff disciplinary, performance and attitude problems. A huge time saver for you.

Additional Resource #2 - 6 x HR Employment Online Courses

Immediate, on demand access to six thorough, online HR courses (with more constantly added), including Employment Tribunal Compensation, Chat GPT for HR Professionals, Deconstructing TUPE, Changing Terms & Conditions, Unconscious Bias At Work and Handling Grievances.

Additional Resource #3 - Free listing on the Register of Investigators

Advertise your professional investigations service in our member's portal.

Additional Resource #4 - Significant discounts on sets of policies, contracts, and other courses.

Get member discounts on my Getting Redundancy Right and HR Policies products as well as other price reductions as new products are released.

▶ WWW.HRINNERCIRCLE.CO.UK ◀

I'm So Confident Joining The HR Inner Circle Is The Right Decision For You, Here's My

NO LIMITS

GUARANTEE

Take action and join the HR Inner Circle **now**.

If you're not 100% satisfied with your investment, you can cancel at ANY time.

Just tell us, and your membership will end immediately. No long-term contracts. No notice periods. No fuss.

I'm comfortable doing this because I know once you join, you'll find the support, the information and the strategies so useful, you'll never want to leave.

Before you decide though, let me be very clear about membership of the HR Inner Circle.

It's only for ambitious and dedicated HR professionals who want to accelerate and increase their impact by plugging into an HR ecosystem with its finger firmly on the pulse of what's working right now in HR.

If you're just plodding along and are content with just getting by, then this is probably not for you.

But if you're drawn to benefiting from standing shoulder to shoulder with some of the giants in the HR community who will help you solve your toughest problems, then joining the HR Inner Circle is the RIGHT decision for you.

Join here now:

▶ WWW.HRINNERCIRCLE.CO.UK ◀

JOIN TODAY

Daniel Barnett

P.S. Remember when you join you get unrestricted access to the private Facebook group, the monthly magazine delivered direct to your door, the monthly audio seminar, regular free books, templates, checklists and resources, on-demand video courses, over 100 audio seminars and back copies of magazines, live interactive Q&A sessions with a lawyer, focused monthly huddles with other HR professionals, a free ticket to the annual conference, your personal concierge plus a bunch of additional resources…